T0408849

My Vesak
Day of Buddha

Written by Priya Kumari
Illustrated by Urvashi Dubey

Eternal Tree Books

Buddhism began in India and then spread to various parts of Asia. It is based on the teachings of the Buddha, who was born more than 2500 years ago as a prince in today's Nepal.

His name was Siddhartha. He left all the luxuries of a royal life behind to search for the truth and to find answers to his questions about life and suffering.

After years of learning and meditation, he gained enlightenment and became the Buddha, which means "*The Enlightened One*".

Vesak is celebrated by millions of Buddhists around the world to honor the life and teachings of the Buddha. Different Asian countries have their own unique ways of celebrating this holiday.

When Asians immigrated to countries like the United States and Canada, they brought this holiday tradition with them.

In India and Tibet, it is more popularly known as Buddha Purnima. Purnima means a full moon day, and the name Vesak comes from the Sanskrit word Vaishakha, which refers to a month of India's traditional calendar. Vesak Day typically occurs in April or May, with specific dates varying across countries.

Many Names For One Holiday

This special holiday has many names in different regions of Asia. Some examples are Buddha Purnima, Buddha Day, Buddha Jayanti, Saga Dawa, Wesak, and Full Moon of Kasun. No matter what this holiday is called, they all celebrate the Buddha!

Vesak Marks Three Important Events in the Life of Buddha

The first significant event is the birth of Siddhartha. His mother, Queen Maya, was traveling to visit her parents when she stopped at the beautiful gardens of Lumbini in Nepal. There, Siddhartha was born!

The baby prince immediately took seven steps, and seven lotus flowers sprang from beneath his feet.

The second important event is when Siddhartha attained enlightenment under the Bodhi Tree which is in Bodh Gaya, India. One day, Siddhartha left his palace to meditate. He wanted to understand why people suffer and feel sad. He meditated for a long time, facing many challenges and temptations.

But on one special night called Vesak, when the moon was full, something amazing happened. As Siddhartha meditated, he learned important truths about life and sadness, and how people can find happiness and be free of sadness. This special moment is called enlightenment. After this, Siddhartha was known as Buddha.

The third event, just as important, is Parinirvana. This event commemorates Buddha's passing away in Kushinagar, India. It marks his attainment of the ultimate goal—being free from the cycle of birth, death, and rebirth.

Vesak Day typically occurs in April or May, with specific dates varying across countries. The festivities commence on the first day of the Vesak month and conclude on the 15th day of the month, which is the full moon day.

During this holy month, we focus on deepening our spiritual practice, reflecting on the teachings of the Buddha, and fostering qualities of compassion, generosity, and mindfulness.

Temples are our special places of worship where we get together and meditate.

We make paper lanterns to decorate our homes and temples. We also put a piece of paper with our written wishes inside these lanterns and hang them in the temples.

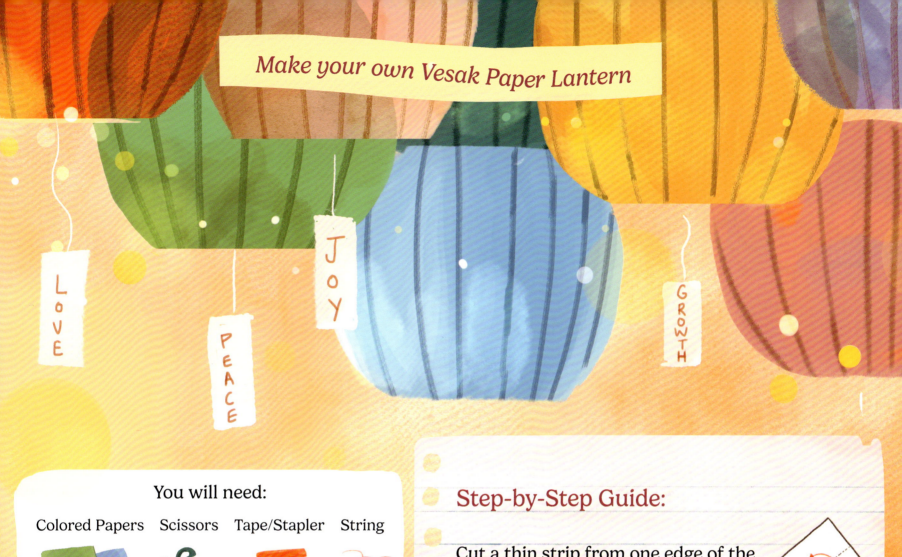

Make your own Vesak Paper Lantern

You will need:

Colored Papers	Scissors	Tape/Stapler	String

Don't forget to add your wishes!

Step-by-Step Guide:

Cut a thin strip from one edge of the square paper for the handle.

Fold the remaining paper in half.

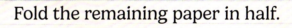

Cut evenly-spaced cuts from the folded side and leave at least an inch at the top

Unfold the paper and shape it into a cylinder. Secure the edges with tape or a stapler.

Attach the strip of paper for the handle and add a string for hanging.

We make Vesak holiday cards for our friends and family. We make Buddhist flags for the procession that we have on the big day of Vesak.

The Buddhist flag has five special colors:
Blue—stands for compassion
Yellow—reminds us of the Middle Path
Red—shows blessings from practice
White—represents the purity of Dhamma
Orange—shines with wisdom

It is said that Buddha's body emanated these bright colors when he attained enlightenment.

On Vesak morning, as the sun is about to rise, we go to the temple to raise the Buddhist flag in a special ceremony. As the flag is raised up the pole, we join together in singing holy hymns. Chanting together at this early hour, we feel the powerful sense of gratitude and humility on this sacred day.

Our voices praise the Three Jewels of Buddhism—the Buddha, the Dharma (his teachings), and the Sangha (his disciples).

PEACE

Inside the temple, there are large bowls filled with water and flowers. Buddha statues stand in a bowl. We use ladles to gently pour holy water over the statues. This shows our respect for Buddha.

The statue of baby Buddha, as he appeared at birth, has his left hand towards the ground and the right hand towards the sky. This represents how he connects the earth with the sky. This act of pouring of water is sacred and symbolizes Buddha's first bath on his birthday.

In Japan, they also have a flower festival called Hana Matsuri. It takes place when the cherry blossoms are in bloom. They pour Amacha on the statue's head with a ladle. Amacha is made from a variety of herbal tea leaves and has a sweet taste. Everyone takes sips of this holy water. This tea helps prevent allergies too.

We also offer a bowl of rice cooked in milk to Buddha. It marks the last meal Buddha had before enlightenment. At the temple, we light oil lamps and joss sticks and offer flowers.

We watch the oil lamps and joss sticks slowly burn down. The flowers start to wilt. This reminds us that nothing lasts forever.

Just like the lamps and joss sticks, our lives do not last forever. This is an important message from Buddha.

Life is temporary and passes quickly.

Remembering this helps us focus on being kind and caring because that is what lasts forever in people's heart.

Outside the temple, our spiritual teachers lead the processions and we walk along with them. We meditate with them and chant 'Paritta' (verses of protective blessings).

Everyone who visits the temple are offered food and tea. We also donate food. This is a reminder to practice generosity. When we are generous, we give our time, love, and possessions to help people. This is a key teaching of Buddha, and we try to practice generosity in our daily lives.

Thousands of paper lanterns, clay diyas or candles light up the evening. By lighting these, we light up our hearts as well as the world.

In this way, the celebration also offers an opportunity in which we reflect on Buddhist virtues, teachings, principles, and life. The light spreading out from these symbolizes Buddha imparting his wisdom to people and bringing light to the world.

In South Korea, they celebrate Vesak with a festive and beautiful lotus lantern parade. It has thousands of lotus-flower-shaped lanterns, cool huge dragons, illuminated lotus flower, and an enormous Buddha statue. These lanterns are made of special Korean paper called Hanji. Buddhist monks chant and perform traditional dances.

The lotus flower is a symbol of purity, spiritual growth, and loyalty. Just as a lotus blooms beautifully above the mud and water, a person can grow and become wiser, even through difficult times. It shows how, with love and dedication, we can rise above challenges and become our best selves.

The streets in Colombo, Sri Lanka, are decorated with pandals on this day. Pandals are temporary stages and huge board-like structures with illustrations of Buddha's life and stories from his previous birth.

In Myanmar, Buddhists carry clay pots filled with water to the sacred Bodhi trees and gently pour water on them.

This tradition honors the Maha-Bodhi tree, under which Prince Siddhartha meditated and attained enlightenment, becoming the Buddha.

Dharamshala, located in India, is home to the official residence of the Dalai Lama. The Tsuglagkhang Complex in Dharamshala, with its natural beauty and spiritual significance, is a special place to celebrate and reflect on the spirit of Buddha Purnima.

The main door of Swayambhu, a temple in Nepal, is opened only on Vesak day. Therefore, people from all around the world come to this place to mark this special day. Vesak in Nepal is more of a national festival than a religious festival because it is celebrated by non-Buddhists as well. Almost everyone goes to the temple in the morning.

Indonesia is home to the world's largest Buddhist temple, and one of the religion's holiest sites, the Borobudur Temple in Central Java. A unique ritual that is performed here is the Pindapata where thousands of monks circle the structure, while praying, to receive charity and blessings for the Indonesian people.

Kong Meng San Phor Kark See Monastery, Singapore, is where you'll see devotees practise the two-hour-long "three-step, one-bow" ritual, taking steps on both knees, bowing at every third step as they pray for world peace, personal blessings, and repentance.

Buddha's birthday is a time of celebration, feasts, lanterns, charity, and generosity. Joyous parades of musicians, dancers, floats, and dragons are common throughout Asia.

It is a light to the path towards creating a world that is peaceful, where everyone is equal and respected. Buddhism teaches us Dana (generosity), Sila (virtue), and Bhavana (mental development).

OM MANI PADME HUM

Om (ohm)

Om is the sound or the vibration of the universe. This sound is the most important of all; but in the context of chanting and mantras, it is meant to destroy attachments to ego and establish generosity.

Ma (mah)

Removes the attachment to jealousy and establishes ethics.

Ni (nee)

Removes the attachment to desire and establishes patience.

Pad (pahd)

Removes the attachment to prejudice and establishes perseverance.

Me (meh)

Removes the attachment to possessiveness and establishes concentration.

Hum (hum)

Removes the attachment to hatred and establishes wisdom.

"Dedicated to those who walk the path of wisdom and compassion." —PK

"To my dearest Jiji, may you discover the wonders of cultures and the wisdom of faiths." —UD

Copyright © 2025 by Eternal Tree Books

All rights reserved. No part of this book may be reproduced or transmitted in any form or by any means, electronic or mechanical, including photocopying or recording, or by any information and retrieval systems without the written permission of the publisher, except where permitted by law.

To request permissions, please contact at info@eternaltreebooks.com

ISBN: 978-1-953384-45-4 (hardcover)
Library of Congress Control Number: 2024950664
First edition 2025

Published by Eternal Tree Books LLC

www.eternaltreebooks.com

Scan for Free Educator Guide